T0130183

THE
MESSAGE
BOY

THE
MESSAGE
BOY

Messages From Spirit

JOHN W. NANT

At time of writing John lived on the gold
coast of Queensland Australia.

THE MESSAGE BOY
MESSAGES FROM SPIRIT

iUniverse books may be ordered through booksellers or by contacting:

iUniverse
1663 Liberty Drive
Bloomington, IN 47403
www.iuniverse.com
1-800-Authors (1-800-288-4677)

Because of the dynamic nature of the Internet, any web addresses or links contained in this book may have changed since publication and may no longer be valid. The views expressed in this work are solely those of the author and do not necessarily reflect the views of the publisher, and the publisher hereby disclaims any responsibility for them.

Any people depicted in stock imagery provided by Thinkstock are models, and such images are being used for illustrative purposes only.
Certain stock imagery © Thinkstock.

ISBN: 978-1-4917-8103-6 (sc)
ISBN: 978-1-4917-8102-9 (e)

Library of Congress Control Number: 2015917335

Print information available on the last page.

iUniverse rev. date: 12/01/2015

This book is dedicated to all of those in spirit who come with love and light, help, guidance and healing to all living beings. Also to those friends whom help me daily on my journey.

May the Love and Light be with you brighter and stronger than ever before

John Nant

Acknowledgement

Many thanks to Carrie Anne St Clair who started me off on this amazing journey

Also to Iris Beaumont who spent many a healing session with me as we exchanged spiritual views also to my wife who put up with me and my way out ideas and theories. I would never have ever reached this far without her love and support thank you I love you dearly

Also to my many spirit guides, teachers, helpers, and healers. Thank you absolutely amazing.

Everything written in this book is the absolute truth and every experience has been written as it happened

Introduction

Is life continuous? For many years I believed the physical body was who we really are and when the time came we departed this planet, died, fell of the perch, karked it, passed away and many other saying with similar meanings, in other words goodbye to life

Then one day I woke up early to go to work (I was 18 yrs old). Then all of a sudden I felt that I didn't need to get up and go at all because my boss Tim had just had a heart attack. Just then I heard the phone ring and my mother answered it. A couple of minutes later my mother came into my bedroom and said,you can stay in bed if you want there is no work today Tim has had a heart attack. For many years I wondered. How did I know about Tim

Many years later whilst reading the newspaper an add stood out at me regarding an international known psychic. Not ever being interested in that part of life before, I felt that for some reason or other it was necessary for me to visit this lady. This lady was on talk back radio and also touring NZ, Australia. So I went to visit this lady and to my amazement told me that I had three children, was divorced, lived close to the great barrier reef, which at that time I was living at Airlie Beach in the Whitsundays

Queensland Australia (This meeting was in New Zealand at the time by the way) This lady then continued on to explain to me how I was going to re marry,hang on a minute I said I sat up straight and replied. Not me. She looked at me and smiled then said whether you think you are or not you are. So I just went along with what she was saying and let her continue. What came out next really surprised me. You are going to be helping people with natural healing also teaching and writing a book. As I looked at her in disbelief she replied yes and its not teaching about building Sailing or Rugby Union,I replied, I don't know about much else so you've got to be kidding me?

By the way I had not told her about Building Sailing or Rugby Union as that is what I know about and do most of the time

No she replied you are, saying it in a way as don't disbelieve in what I am saying because I know what I know okay. That's how it is

So after that lot I just listened

Within the next few weeks I was really intrigued about the session also other certain incidents that were happening in my life. How did I know about Tim how did this lady know all about me I had never ever met her before

(Buy the way I am now very happily married and live on the Gold Coast

Queensland Australia the lady had told me also that my wife will have dark hair and she has.)

My next experience in this amazing new field to me was I went to a meditation class in Coolangatta, on the border of Queensland and New South Wales my first meditation class and the teachers name was Carrie. I just sat very quietly just listening to all talking Carrie stood up and said Hello everyone thank you for coming tonight we are going to have a past life meditation. Well I just went along with what Carrie had just said thinking to myself don't know much about this lot but never mind it will be a different experience something new

Well we had the meditation and I saw myself on a big white horse going (Flying Actually) around different parts of the world and then the universe. Wow absolutely amazing was my reaction how interesting. When the meditation was finished Carrie called me The Universal Traveller and then said your horse looked beautiful and what did I think of my life in England in the days of the Highway Men which I had seen also. I looked at Carrie Gobsmacked to say the least and said Amazing Carrie had seen my whole meditation, everywhere I had been she told me about it

Since then I have seen myself in many lifetimes, also I have seen how many of my lives finished. Many of the lifetimes ended quite gruesome, but it didn't worry me as

I knew I was here in this lifetime fit and well. I also now realize how I seem to be very interested in certain ways of life (been there before) so with meditation to me, being so interesting enjoyable and feeling so good after each one I started meditating everyday, which I did for seven years. Now days I seem to switch in and out of that state several times each day automatically

Healing

In the seven years of meditating daily I started to study and learn about healing and the many different ways and methods. It is quite amazing how many methods there are I tried a few of them and in the end I started doing what came to me automatically

After a while I started having people come around home asking for certain advice on how to meditate and how to invoke the Healing Energy

It is amazing how the universe works for here is me learning and all of a sudden people are asking me about certain subjects and also what I am experiencing at this point in time (A friend of a friend explained to me what do you do was the catch phrase from many of the people who came to see me

Then they would say. I would like to learn if you could teach me please as I have been interested for a long time but don't seem to be able to get started.

So I then started my own meditation and healing classes.

Over the years there has been many amazing experiences and stories so I thought I would add a few of these in this book

Life Experiences

Louise came to see me one day about having a healing as she had heard from someone else that I had helped a friend of hers. As I started the healing I sensed a sadness between her and her grandmother. Louise went on to tell me that she was a nurse and spent a lot of time with elderly patients. Quite often she would have flashbacks of her and her grandmother. When she was little and growing up her grandmother was her favourite person in the whole wide world.

When turning seventeen her grandmother had spoken to her about wearing a very short skirt and a low cut top, remarking that she looked very tarty and would only invite trouble from the wrong type of males. So with these remarks her grandmother was not her favourite person anymore and so therefore gave the grandmother a verbal serving and walked away. Never to talk to her again. Many years later while travelling overseas Louise received a phone call from her mother explaining to her that grandma was very sick and would be lucky to be around for too long. Her mother asked her to please come home and see her in case she never see's her ever again so Louise hopped on a plane from London and came back to Australia to see her grandma. Louise landed in Brisbane then caught a bus back to the gold coast just as she arrived back on the Gold Coast she received a message from her mother that grandma had just passed away,so close but so far away

As Louise was in tears explaining her story I mentioned that somebody in spirit was standing at the end of table. All of a sudden an outburst of emotion and more tears 'Its Grandma' I have seen her many times in spirit and wish that I could talk to her and say sorry. I passed on a message to her from Grandma saying please do not cry and please do not be sorry for it was her fault for speaking out of line (By the way this session is 28 yrs after the actual original argument) then out of the blue Louise explained to me that she can see and talk to spirit sometimes but has never been able to talk to Grandma so I asked Grandma if she would like to speak to Louise direct and if she could. Then I asked Louise if she would like to speak to Grandma direct as my spirit guides were going to tune them into each other if they would like. With a yes from both parties I then asked Louise to please listen for Grandma and that way it would save me transferring messages well Louise gave me the thumbs up and her and Grandma talked for around 20 - 25 minutes. As I stood there I could see Louise laughing then crying-laughter again, big smiles, more tears and also as with Grandma in spirit and as they were solving all there indifferences they were both very very happy and then all of sudden Grandma just disappeared into a beautiful white light. Louise then sat up on the table with a big smile and told me how she apologised for being an upstart smarty pants to grandma and how grandma said that she (grandma) should have minded her own business. Then they talked about all of the good times they had. Louise then hopped of the table. Looking 10 years younger,gave me a big hug and off she went

(Please remember this story could happen to many of us) and then live in regret for many years the following Christmas I received a thank you card and some very nice Christmas candles from Louise

Many years ago I decided to go to the mind body spirit festival in Brisbane. So on the train from the Gold Coast I went, as I walked through the main entrance I received a message from spirit to go down the allyway of stalls on the right hand side of the building. So I did. As I was walking through all the stalls and looking I received another message. Please keep walking turn left at second isle then turn left again so I followed the message and there was a lady who was a friend of mine John she called out fancy seeing you here right at this time. Would you like a quick cup of coffee as the next 20 minutes is all I have spare all day. This particular lady is a reader and a very busy one at that. I thanked my messenger and then off we went for coffee and had a very interesting talk all about the many different thing that seem to be happening to many people in life at the moment, mainly the spiritual awareness of many that have never been interested in this subject before, just thought I would put this paragraph in letting people know to be aware of any messages that might be coming to them from spirit with love - light.

At the same mind body spirit festival an hour or so later I came across a store full of crystals and one very big crystal bed. The bed was a four poster and on top of each post was a different crystal, all of them around 100 millimetres long and around 75 millimetres in width the first crystal I looked at I thought wow you are beautiful. To my amazement from the crystal came, so are you love and light. So I looked at the second crystal and I received the word peace. The third crystal on top of the post I received the word healing, and the fourth crystal I received happiness.

Well I just stood there gazing in awe of what had just happened. A lady came up to me and asked if I was okay. With this I replied yes thank you I was just looking at the crystals on the top of each bed post, and I received love, peace, healing happiness wow she replied that is amazing because I tuned the four crystals in at 7-00 this morning as love peace healing happiness. You are a lucky man apparently the crystals told her what I do and we then continued to talk for quite some time. Funny enough as we were talking, within 10-15 minutes her stall was full of people all looking at the crystals on top of the four bedposts

One time my wife and I were up in North Queensland. When a lady asked me what do I do for work. I explained to her about healing and mediumship so she booked in for a session the following day explaining about a few aches and pains that she had been having for quite some time and they didn't seem to go away. I held her hand and explained that a man of smallish build was in the room with a big smile on his face. He had a green chequered Scottish style kilt on and matching socks pulled up just below the knees with a little tassel on each sock. With this the lady smiled and replied that sounds like my dad, I have been thinking of him a lot lately as soon as the lady mentioned about her Dad the man in the kilt starting nodding and replied that is correct, I am her dad. He had one very big happy smiley face as I received more messages from her dad and passed them on the more confirmation she had, that it was definitely her dad

I also then received messages from my Dad for myself. Then the lady explained that she felt that she was talking to her dad direct, I double checked all the information and she was, she seemed to have been tuned into her dad direct which she talked then to him for around 15-20 minutes. One minute she was laughing and then crying tears rolling down her face, and then instantly burst out laughing. They were having a great chat while they were talking away to each other. My dad who was a motor mechanic whilst here on the earth plane went on to explain to me about certain items that needed attention or fixing on the motor of our yacht. So the next week or two that I did I took heed of what he said and with very good advice I got our motor fixed. (Thank you dad) it certainly saved a big hassle out at sea.

Then returning to the lady she then replied that her dad was now gone and not only that all her aches and pains were also gone. She hopped off the chair and gave my a great big hug, I then said please go and have a look at yourself in a mirror as you look 10 years younger. Off to the mirror she went and after 5 minutes came back with the biggest smile. I do too thank you.

By the way the lady did not stop talking about what had just happened for quite some time I still see this lady regularly just to talk and is still one very happy lady

A few years ago my wife and I were renting a two story house which we lived in for 4 years when we decided to move out the next door neighbour asked me if he could cut down a certain tree which was close to his boundary as the leaves kept dropping into his swimming pool. I explained that it was not my tree to have the say to whether he could cut it down or not. I then went down to the tree and looked how close it was to the boundary I then realised what he was talking about. The next moment was amazing the tree said to me, that a particular branch could be taken off as it was the one dropping the leaves into the pool, but please do not cut it down for twenty minutes.

I went over to the fence and called out to the neighbour and said that he could cut down a certain branch but not for twenty minutes. He smiled and looked at me as if I was a little weird then replied see you in twenty minutes.

15 minutes later I went back down to the tree looked at the branch and it was alive with little insects all climbing down from the branch to be cut off and onto a different

part of the tree that was staying. I stood there watching all this happening until the last one left that branch. I then heard thank you your twenty minutes is up. I looked at my watch and it was exactly twenty minutes. At that moment the neighbour called out are you ready for me to come over and cut the branch down.

Yes was my reply, totally in awe of what had just happened.

Several years ago I had a dream about being in New Zealand. I was going whitebaiting at a place called Tangimoana on the Rangatikei River, I was at a certain sandhill beside the water about 300 metres from the river entrance to the sea I had a wooden box with a gauze bottom and in it was lots and lots of whitebait (whitebait is a small clear fish and a delicacy to many people) About 3-4 months later I decided to fly to New Zealand and go to Tangimoana and go whitebaiting. I borrowed a net and off I went to the river. When I got there I saw this certainSandhill as a landmark. There was 3 other people with me also. The 3 people said we are going to the entrance of the river.

I then explained that I am going up river to that Sandhill and Ill fish beside the hill. They laughed and then went on to tell me that nobody has been catching any fish up there for a long time

(I hadn't told them about my dream) So off we went in different directions

Well in about 1 hour later one of the other persons came to see how I was going. I lifted my net out of the water and had quite a few whitebait in it. My very good friend said, that's more than the 3 of us have got so far between us. I smiled and said go and have a look in the box.

Well he looked at me smiled and off he went, within 20 minutes there were 4 of us fishing beside the Sandhill. We all stayed for around 4 hours fishing and funny enough I was the only one catching them, much to the disappointment of the other 3, I had a couple of pounds and they were lucky if they even had a cup full between them

About a year ago a lady came to me regarding a healing session for a very painful neck. While she was on the healing table I saw her as an Egyptian Priestess wearing Golden Headware I then asked her if she believed in past lives

Oh yes definitely she replied, why do you ask I then explained to her what I had just seen, she then laughed and said,I always thought that I was an Egyptian Priestess, even when I was a little girl I always read books on Egypt and the pyramids. Also about a year ago a clairvoyant had explained to her that she had been in Egypt in a previous life. I then went on to explain about what she was and what she did in the Egyptian days of that lifetime. Just as we had finished talking,the lady sat upright and said I don't know what that was to do with my physical body in this life but my neck if now fine and all the aches and pains have gone. She looked at me with a great big smile replied amazing and then left.

Early on this year a lady rang and explained that her and her neighbour had what they called a nasty spirit in there units. So one I night I arranged to meet her after her work as she was very busy 7 days a week running her own health food business. She explained that her dog won't go into the laundry and out the back door. So when I got to her unit I met the dog and I starting walking towards the laundry,the dog put its head into the room and then started crouching down on all 4 legs and then started whimpering. (It was a little dog and very timid) I then went into the laundry and there on top of the hot water cylinder was the spirit of a male. I looked at him and told him it was time for him to go home to the light. All of a sudden he just said nearly every swear word that I had heard before and maybe a few that I hadn't, and then told me where to go in no uncertain terms. I just looked at him and said tough luck mate you're going and that's that whether you like it or not. Then another list of swear words came from him, and he replied after that not me not going anywhere get lost. You'll see, smart aase well I replied the ladies want you out and it is their place not yours and yes we will see.

After 10 minutes of discussions and pursuetions he disappeared in a big flash of light.

After having a cup of coffee and a few biscuits I went back into the laundry and called the dog. The lady came into the laundry and also coaxed the dog to come in as well

As the dog came into the laundry the first thing it did was to look up to the top of the hot water cylinder and then it walked right through the room and out the back door

Not worried anymore it turned around and walked back inside again. The spirit was gone and apparently what happened was that in the middle of the night the wayward spirit was making a noise which sounded like marbles being rolled across the tile floor and waking everyone up

A month later I was on the phone and was told, no noise and the dog was happy to go into the laundry

Two years ago a construction worker came to see me regarding a few aches and pains he had (as he put it) He was having trouble with his neck and back and also a few emotional troubles,he layed on the healing table and we carried on talking about his discomforts when all of a sudden I saw a man in spirit sitting on a Harley Davidson Motor Bike right in the centre of the room. I asked my spirit guides who he was and was it alright for him to be here during this session. My main guide said to please listen to what he had to say as he is a friend of the man on the table, and all is well as I looked at the man in spirit again he would have been at least 6 ft tall and about 17-18 stone in weight he was sitting on his Harley revving it up. He had a big bushy beard tattoos on both arms and a great big smile. As I was about to ask him his name he said my name is Bruce and I was a friend of the man on the table but please don't tell him my name as he will know anyway so I turned to my client and explained to him what I had just seen in the middle of the healing room. I also explained to him that the man on the Harley said he was a friend of yours, with this my client looked straight at me and replied that's probably Bruce he got hit and killed by a truck about 15 years ago. I then turned to Bruce and he was nodding his head in a yes manner. Thats me was the reply and then Bruce disappeared in a large flash of very bright light. I explained to my client what had just happened and also that just before he went he said to say thank you for being his friend and thank you for organising much of the funeral party for him. He was sorry for the tears he had caused you and all his friends but please do not worry about him as it is more beautiful here than you could ever imagine. But please do not try to get here just yet, as it is not yet your time.

The next moment my client got up off the table and replied. Yes I did organise, the after funeral party and we gave him a great send off

Also what is amazing is all my aches and pains have gone and I always wondered what happened to Bruce. What appeared to have happened was that my client was holding onto the grief for all of those years and now he knew that life goes on after the physical body is finished on this plane. He shook my hand, said thank you and walked out the door saying wow, wow wow.

About 5 years ago a lady was explaining to me how her son has an invisible friend and that her son talks to him all the time. She also said that she was a single mum and her 10 yr old son set a place for his invisible friend at the table every day. I then explained to her that setting a place at the table is not a very good idea. For the reason being it could keep the spirit around, plus all spirits are not as nice as each other, not until they have gone home to the light. Many of them can be mischievous. I was explaining to her that the mischievous ones can sometimes persuade young humans into doing silly things as going down to a creek or a river for a swim and try to get them to swim across to the other side, also they often try to talk the physical humans into walking across the road at a very dangerous time.

All of a sudden she went oh my gosh I have told my son off twice in the last 2 weeks for swimming in the river. He is not allowed to go anywhere near it without her being around, and he has never done that before, when I tell him off she replied he just says Johnny said its okay. With this reply I asked her son whereabouts is his friend Johnny at the moment. He replied he is sitting on the floor over there (which was about 5 metres from the boy.) I then said to the ladys son please ask Johnny to go to the light. The reply from Johnny was no, so I asked the boy to ask Johnny for the second time please go to the light the same answer was given No.

So I then said to the boy please ask Johnny for the 3rd and last time please go into the light or he shall be taken. (Universal Law states if you ask a spirit to leave 3 times and it does not go it will be taken by light beings of the higher order)

With this the little boy asked Johnny to go to the light. The reply then from Johnny was what is the light and instantly the 10 yr old boy said to his mum Wow a Great big Angel came and took Johnny away straight into the middle of a big Bright Light, can I go outside and play now. About 20 minutes later the 10 yr old comes in asking for a biscuit. I said to him have you seen Johnny around. He replied no he then looked around the room and then up at the ceiling where the bright light had been and then replied. Johnny's not coming back he's with his grandma and granddad can I go back outside and play now. I then looked at the lady and remarked that it is finished, she just sat there speechless for around 5 minutes and then we had coffee and biscuits

A very good friend asked me a few years ago if I could send healing to the young daughter of a very good friend of his. His friend was an officer in the police force and his 5 yr daughter had been diagnosed will a rare disease. The parents had just been told that she may only have a few months to live so with this news they decided to take a trip to England to see the little girls grandparents

I went into my healing room and sat beside my table. I then tuned into the necessary energies for a healing session after asking all concerned, the parent, said yes as much as possible please as we love our daughter very much but please ask our daughter (This is all on a Spiritual level by the way) I did this and the daughter replied No thank you not yet also by the way I am not going anywhere so please try again next week.

So 1 week later I sat beside the healing table and asked permission again from the parents and the daughter to be able to send healing. This time the parents said yes and the daughter replied yes also. As I was asking for the Universal healing energy of Love-Light the daughters spirit came and layed on the table. She then said to me thank you I am open to receive as much healing as possible. But by the way I am not going anywhere for quite some time for my time here on earth is not up yet.

I then saw a very bright light over the whole table and over the 5 year olds spirit. It was very intense, then it came brighter with a big flash and was gone. I then heard thank you from the 5 yrs old girl and also from the parents.

It is absolutely amazing to think that these people were in England all the time and I was on the Gold Coast Queensland Australia

This little girl is now a 13 yr old teenager still alive and well. I also heard a few months ago from my friend that she was a typical teenager as well.

Around seven years ago a gentleman whom I had met whilst talking with others, and on the street just along from where I was living, asked me what I did for work. I explained to him natural healing. What type he asked. Tuning into the Universal healing energy's mainly I replied. When the other people I was speaking to left he asked me if he could bring his 3 yr old son to me for a session. He said that his son had not spoken one word to him or his wife ever. He said him and his wife were very concerned. The boy would watch TV and smile and that was all. I said yes to him but that I do not guarantee any particular results as there are many attributing factors involved

The next day his wife brought the 3 yr old boy around home introduced herself and the boy to me, then said please see if you can help in any way. So I got the lady to lay on the healing table with her son beside her. The lady was doing the talking and the little boy just kept staring at me. After channeling the healing energy and information gathering re both of them the little boy started getting restless it was like his energy had doubled since he first arrived. Getting a little too restless I explained that it would be of benefit to finish now and if they would both be able to come back in a weeks time. One week later same again the lady was doing the talking and the little boy just stared at me. I asked a few questions and then proceeded with another round of channeling healing energy. The little boy stayed on the table about twice as long as the first session and then slid of the table, still no words just hanging on to his mother. I explained that I felt it would be of benefit if they came again in one weeks time. One week later they both arrived at the house and the lady said that the boy seemed more at ease and relaxed at home but still no talking

So on the table for the third time they got. After about half an hour the little boy sat up and looked at me is it to say that's enough I want to go home. His mother tried to get him to lay down again but to no avail. I just said to the lady if you feel like coming again please do so, but only if you feel that you would like to. Two days later there was a knock on the door about 7-00 pm while we were having dinner. I got up from the table and went to the front door there was the little boys father. He just looked at me and said sorry to bother you but what colour do you prefer red or blue I replied I love blue the most as it is my favourite colour (I love most colours) why is that. He just looked at me and Ill be back in a moment please wait at the door. So I waited at the front door wondering what on earth is going on

The next moment he returned with the most beautiful dark blue with gold embroidery Indian blanket. What's this about I asked. He looked at me with tears in his eyes and said our son came up to me last night when I was on the couch he put his arms around my neck and said I love you daddy,we both stood at the front door with tears running down our cheeks just talking. He insisted that I keep the blanket. I kept saying no its okay you keep it is too beautiful to give away anyway in the end he wouldn't take no for an answer, so now I have one very beautiful blanket with gold embroidery and gold tassels right around it. To finish of this story

Two weeks later the mother and the little boy came around to our house. I was standing out the front on the footpath at the time. The little boy looked at me and said 'Hello John.' Well I nearly tell over backwards amazing he stood there with his mum with a great big smile as if he had been talking for year's. That's great I said to the mum isn't it? she just replied with a great big smile you haven't got an on-off button have you because he just doesn't stop talking we just laughed and then they went on their way

A few months ago whilst in NTH Queensland Australia my jeep Cherokee 4 wheel drive vehicle started making a very horrible rattling noise. Wow I said to my friend who was travelling with me at that time can you hear that, he replied sure can doesn't sound to good at all. So I stopped the vehicle and as I went to lift up the bonnet (or hood) a message from my father in spirit came through 'Can't fix this one yourself boy needs to be fixed properly please take it to a garage, it is a collapsed water pump bearing and it will cost you between five and six hundred dollars,I must admit I was not happy about the pump and the cost but I was very blessed to hear from Dad, as he was a motor mechanic whilst here on the earth plane in the physical,so I drove the jeep to a garage of choice and explained to the owner of the garage what had happened. He lifted up the bonnet and said it is your water pump and you will require a new one please come back tomorrow around 4-30 pm as it will have to ordered in from out of town and could take up to two days to get it. So 4-30 the next day I went to pick up the jeep,it was repaired and ready to drive away the cost was $540-00. The owner asked me what I do for a job as he had seen one of my cards inside the vehicle. I explained to him about receiving messages from those who are now in spirit. He laughed and replied. What about me is there any messages for me, smiling to himself. As a matter of fact there is if you would like to hear it there is one from your father who happens to be standing right beside you. Well, the laughter stopped and the smile turned to a smirk. Go ahead he replied I actually don't believe it anyway but see what you come up with. Over the next 5 to 10 minutes I gave him the exact words his father said to me. You've got to be kidding he replied only my Dad and I know about those things that you just said. Well I better get back to work. He was totally shocked that there was life after the physical. His young mechanic said could there be any for me. I replied if you would like to I will see as I always ask for permission on both sides first I asked him to close his eyes and who was coming to mind. He replied a friend of mine from a couple of years ago. Then he replied, I can see a rope and a girl which was his friends girlfriend.

I then said to him your friend has just asked me to get you to explain the story now please open your eyes. The young mechanic then went on to tell me how his friend had hung himself and that everybody blamed his girlfriend for it and still did. When the young mechanic had finished his story, his friend in spirit then went on to explain how it wasn't his girlfriends fault, it was his own because it was his choice not hers. Please let everyone know and please please do not blame her for it anymore. The young mechanic looked at me totally amazed with a few tears in his eyes and replied that is exactly how it was if you come back to this town please come and say Hello I would like to see if there any more messages but I think that is enough for now, Wow.

Several years ago when I first started receiving messages from spirit I would receive messages about certain meditation and healing classes that would be of benefit to me. I was also meditating 3-4 times a day and had joined a spiritual group in Brisbane. I used to go to these groups twice a week. After going for about two years I was asked by spirit to relay a message to all of those in the room, about 30 people at the time, so I asked all the people and yes was the reply. So I started relaying the message from spirit to everyone and the messages went on for about 10 minutes. At the end of the messages I looked at everyone and they all looked in complete shock.

The lady running the class said to me do you remember what was said. No I don't I replied the messages were for you all not for me and most of the time when this happens I do not retain the message. Well she replied would you like to know what was said. Yes thank you if you feel like I need to know. Well she said, you just said that the people on the committee of these classes and this group and also the organiser plus the top lady of these classes and group will not be elected again at the next general meeting. Also because they were not spiritually advanced enough to run such a class. Also you told me that I was going to be a grandmother again but this time to my youngest daughter. My daughter is only sixteen years of age and has not even got a boyfriend. So I think your messages are way off the mark and are not correct, to cut a long story short I was then thrown out of this particular group and told never to come back again. Guess what? I received a phone call about 3 months later from the lady who was running the class that particular night (whom I might add is a very nice lady and we ended up as friends) John she said I though that I might let you know my youngest daughter is 3 months pregnant and also the annual general meeting was held last week and all of the committee members like you said never got voted back in again. Neither did Boss Lady. I know you have complete faith in what you receive from spirit and I am sorry that I doubted you. When I am receiving message from those in the light or from the light I know that these messages always come with love so if you are talking with spirit beings from the light, please trust they always come with love & light.

My 1st encounter with seeing spirit about 20 yrs ago I was sailing on my yacht a 32 ft Swanson from the Gold Coast Queensland

Australia up to the Whitsunday Islands a distance of 500 nautical miles I anchored for the night in a bay on an island at the start of the Whitsundays my two friends and I were sitting in the cockpit of the yacht we had dinner and just talked until 11-00 pm then off to bed. I had given my two friends my usual double cabin as the two were the couple, I think one was the new girlfriend of and old flat male if I remember. Around 2-00 am in the morning I awoke with a feeling of someone doing something with my hand. I opened my eyes and to my amazement saw someone in spirit standing right beside me. As I went to speak it moved to the other side of the yacht and leant against the galley bench. I said if you're a good spirit you can stay if not get off my yacht now

(A very different conversation to what I have with spirit nowadays) With this it disappeared out of the cabin and off. But on the way it knocked over my lantern (which was battery powered lucky), from the cockpit seat and down on to the floor

My friend came out of the double cabin and said 'what's going on' I heard a bang is everything OK. When I told him he burst out laughing, you silly old fool I packed the lantern in the cushion so it wouldn't fall out. Well I replied go outside and see for yourself smarty pants. The water is flat like a mirror, so who did it. Oh well so he went outside and when he came back into the cabin he just looked at me shrugged his shoulders there's know way it could off fallen by itself so who care's let all go back to sleep and see what happens. We all woke up in the morning and my friend still couldn't work out or understand how the lantern came out of the cushions as he did not believe in a spirit world nowadays he does and even has even seen them himself

Another amazing experience I have had with a 10 yr old boy, it was regarding hardly speaking to anyone a lady rang me one day and explained that a friend of hers had been to see me regarding a painful neck - shoulders. Apparently the session did wonders for her physical and mental self

The lady then explained that her 10 yr old son was very quiet and reserve. Did not say a lot to others at school and got picked on by others for being so quiet, those at school thought he was a little slow in many ways.

When the boy first came to the house with his mum he put his head down and didn't say a word. The second time he came was a week later he looked at me put his head down again and then muttered Hello. The third time that the boy and his mother came around to the house he looked at me shook my hand and said Hello John

The lady was explaining to me that he used to have lots of dreams about spirit coming into his bedroom at night time. When I explained to him that I can see spirit also he opened up and told me all about his dreams, people he was and still is seeing in spirit. Wow I thought this little guy is tuned into the spirit world big time. I then explained to his mother what was happening and that he was going to be doing healing in the future himself and that he had a very good talent that nobody else knew about after being picked on he wasn't going to tell anyone about it either

About 3 months later the lady rang me up to explain how her son was these days and that he was now in the school drama class. Now days his family and myself are very good friends. Everytime I see them the boy comes and shakes my hand and says hello John, he is still quite reserve in his manner but also a lot more aware of life than most people realize. It will be interesting to see what he does in the future. I get that he will be a very good medium

People are amazing around seven years ago a gentleman came to see me regarding a few physical ailments that he had. He wondered if I could help in anyway, Apparently I had helped a friend of his before. I explained to him as I do to all clients that I do not guarantee results that they are looking for. I will admit that some of the results' I have seen are absolutely amazing

I just look at the universe and say thank you so he arrives with a list of twelve items he explained that the priority on the list was that he had to get up to go to the toilet about ten times every night. His exact words were I feel busting to go to the toilet when I get there I have about three or four drops or drips and that's all. I then go back to bed, wake up about an hour later and do the same again. So I checked out the rest of the list and said you might have to come for three or four sessions. Okay he replied whatever it takes because it is driving me bonkers he hopped up on to the healing table. I did what I do with him which involves finding out various issues which could be the cause of. I then did a healing on him for half an hour and off the table he got. He sat down in his chair and explained to me what he felt and what came to mind during the time on the table. Well he arrived back a week later with his list. Four items were crossed off and he said amazing I only have to go to the toilet once a night and that's about four in the morning and it works great. We finished off the second session and at the end of that session he crossed off another four items from his list. He returned two weeks later and explained how good he felt. Onto the table he got, he was on the table for half an hour and then off he got he looked at me in total amazement and said 'Who told you to fix my arm? I never had that on my list. He crossed of three more items of his list which only left one more I replied what is the story regarding your arm. He lifted his arm straight up into the air and then straightened it. I have not been able to do that for 10 years. I fell of a ladder whilst painting because that was my profession and have been on a disability pension ever since. Also I am not going back to work. I looked at him and replied what are you worried about you have already past retirement age, I then explained to him that it would be of benefit to come back one more time next week. Okay was the reply A week later he never turned up for his appointment but rang twenty minutes after he was supposed to have been here, he then went on to explain that he was not coming back anymore as it didn't work for him. I replied you crossed off eleven items of your list of twelve and maybe the twelve item was going to be cleared today. He just said the twelfth item was what I was after the most. So it doesn't work and then he hung up. So I get the message that sometimes people do not choose to be totally well as there is no talking point for them when they go out and mix with others. Also no sympathy voles from their friends either. But never mind it was his choice and I am a big believer in everyone having their own choice in and about life.

A lady from Townsville Qld rang me one day and explained that her son was having many dreams about drowning and that a man dressed in black seemed to be in every dream. The lady also explained how she was worried as two days before she rang me her son came home from the public swimming pool and told her that he saw a man in black five or six times around the swimming pool. He said that the man was carrying a sign saying 'You are going to drown. Everytime her son looked straight at the man in black the man disappeared so he got a little worried and went home. The lady asked me if I could explain in anyway what was going on. I tuned in on the situation and explained to her what I was receiving. She then replied that she would bring her son to the Gold Coast as they were going on holiday to stay not far from where I was anyway an two weeks time. So two weeks later the boy was at my place and explained the whole story to me from his point of what was happening.

At that moment I saw a man in spirit dressed in black, he was holding up a sign you are going to drown I asked the boy if he could see him. The boy replied, Yes but I don't like him. With this I did not bother to ask the man in black who he was or what was he doing around the boy. I just said to him to leave immediately and go to the light.

He mumbled a whole lot of swear words and told me where to go in no uncertain terms. I just said for the second time just leave and go to the light. He swore at me again and said the boy is going to drown so I replied no he is not and you are going home to the light so leave or you will be taken. He just swore some more shrugged his shoulders and all of a sudden I just saw a large bright flash of light and he was gone my spiritual guides at that time just took him home. All I received from my guides was that the man in black was a trouble maker and who had drowned himself whilst on the earth plane,the boy just looked at me and said I heard and saw all of that, pretty cool and awesome he's gone anything else. No I replied all done. I had a couple of phone calls over the next few years from the lady just letting me know that her son had never had anymore drowning dreams and also had not ever seen the man in black again. To me it was amazing how the young boy could see and hear what was going on in a spirit realm. He was only 11 yrs old

Many years ago my wife and I moved into a unit on the beach front at Main Beach Gold Coast Qld Australia. The unit was fully furnished and was owned by an elderly couple who lived in the same block of units also. Not long after moving there I felt like changing my way of life as far as work was concerned. I received a phone call from a close friend asking if I had time to meet an elderly lady who apparently wanted to meet me. This elderly lady happened to be a very good clairvoyant and had seen me doing something which had intrigued her. I agreed to meet with this lady a week later. When the lady turned up at the front door her exact word were Hello John I don't know why I have too meet you as yet, but I do. I invited her into the unit and we sat at the dining room table. She then started to explain to me who she was and what she did for a living and had been clairvoyant all her life she was now 73 years of age

I just sat there listening to her and was wondering what was going on,she then asked if she could hold my hand which I agreed. From then on she explained to me about what I was going to achieve in the future. She then told me what she had seen me doing Healing, Taking Spiritual classes, Spiritual work and that there was no end to what I could achieve in that field if I chose to follow that path. Straight away I thought

well I was wanting a change anyway and it sounded very interesting,she stood up and said, well now I know why I was asked by spirit to come and meet you. She gave me a big hug and then continued to explain to me how I was going to help people and then the lady said, well must go and she went home. Apparently the lady lived about 1½ hrs drive from me.

A few months after that interesting day the elderly man who owned the unit passed away and the lady (his wife) gave my wife and I all of the furniture in the unit,fridge and all

About seven years after my wife and I had moved out of that unit I was at a mind body spirit festival listening to a guest clairvoyant speaker. There was around 50 people in the room when the speaker said who in the room is John. I have a lady in spirit by the name of Beryl and she keeps calling out John John its Beryl I put my hand up in the air and replied 'I'm John but so did 5 others. The Guest Speaker said you know a Beryl and its something to do with furniture. The other Johns said not me and then I realised it was me for Beryl gave us the furniture from the unit and my wife and I were only talking about it the day before (Wow amazing I thought). The speaker then said that Beryl just wanted to say hello and that she was in spirit now with her family.

So to all those who are reading this please remember we all go home to the light when we have finished with our physical body on the earth plane and have many friends and loved ones in spirit to greet us

A few years ago I had been asked to see a lady in North Queensland if I was ever travelling in that particular area I rang and left a message to ring me when available. About a month later I received a phone call from the lady asking if she could come to my place in two weeks time. How amazing I will actually be in your town in two weeks time so we made an appointment to meet at her house it was a 3½ hr drive for me but never mind I enjoy the drive. When I arrived at her house she looked at me and said I think you are the one. Which one I replied. I keep getting in my sleep that a man is coming into my life to help me,she replied and I think and feel that it is you,straight away I passed a message to her from her mother in spirit. She looked at me and smiled and said Sounds like her but I would like to have more proof. I then relayed another message from her mother, saying you always were a doubting Thomas, so here is something to let you know it is me your mother. When you go out on Friday nights wash behind your ears, have clean underwear on and keep your pants on your hips.

With this the elderly lady replied that's my mum for sure. She used to say that to me every Friday when I was a teenager and only her and I knew that. I then gave her a healing session for half an hour and then I left. I was never told how I was going to help her but I did hear about 3 months later she seemed a whole lot happier

Early in 2014 my wife and I were sailing across the Whitsundays in Queensland Australia on a very beautiful day. Just as the sails on the yacht needed adjusting for the wind change a large school of Dolphins came alongside just swimming and playing. I looked at the lead Dolphin and said you are so beautiful absolutely amazing,all of a sudden I, heard, so are you and enjoy your sail back to the Gold Coast. Goodbye for now

Now that's pretty strange I thought, firstly I wasn't even thinking about going to the Gold Coast and had no intention of moving back there. Simply because we had just moved to the Whitsundays to live there permanently. Guess what we put our house in the Whitsundays up for sale and we now live back on the Gold Coast (not because of what the dolphin said but other circumstances. Not only that, the Dolphins come around the yacht when we go sailing here and also Dolphins come around the yacht nearly every night while we a berthed at the Marina Hunting for food.

Around eight years ago my wife and I went to California for two months. We hired a Volkswagen Combie Campervan and drove from the Redwood forests in the north all the way down to San Diago. Just

Nth of San Diago is an old Cowboy Ranch type settlement. We parked the Combie and started walking from one end of the town to the other. About a quarter of the way along we came across an old saloon. I instantly had a flash of fighting. There were horses raring up in the air. A couple of full on Gun fights and people running everywhere. I stood there for a few minutes watching all of this absolutely amazed. Walking along a bit further there was a plaguard explaining some of the fights the gunfights and other certain antics that went on in those days. Now I thought I have just seen some of them and then all of a sudden I saw quite a few horses in spirit going around and around in the middle of the road and over to the other side of the street. So with this I went over to the other side,there was another plaguard explaining that area used to be the Corral in the 1800s. I also saw people walking around in the type of dresses and clothes of that era low and behold a few shops later and there were photos of the corral, the fights, the horses and also the way the people dressed,a flash from the past must of happened. Absolutely amazing

In that same year as we went to America we also spent five weeks in the UK. Visiting one of the old castles the tour guide was explaining who lived there many years ago. Just as the tour guide started to speak I saw about forty people having a party around a very big table which was covered in food and drinks. I noticed some big glass vases (I thought) on the table. Once the tour guide went off in a different direction I stayed there for a another ten - fifteen minutes just looking at the party going on. As I walked away from that room and past the next room there was a painting that had a lot of the people in it that I had just seen in the previous room. Also in the painting there was some of the fancy vases or jars that I had seen. Going past and into many of the other rooms. Some of them had paintings in them also I then realised that what I thought were vases were actually for filling up different drinks. A very very interesting chapter in my life was starting

I was at a friends house one morning and we happened to be talking about the type of work that I had been doing lately. We were carrying around some furniture when all of a sudden he stopped and asked if I had seen his two children. No I haven't I replied, why is that. Well he replied I am sure that my son keeps seeing and talking to someone in spirit. Either that or he has started talking to himself. I then explained to him how many children see and talk to spirit, but remember not all spirits are what you would call good. That could be why he has been a little smarty pants lately, my friend said. He has been back answering his mother and has started swearing a lot also. With this I replied get them both to come here where we are talking if you like and I will ask them both what is going on. My friend started calling out to his children but neither replied. So my friend and I started walking around his property looking for them. The little girl was playing in the garden and said she thought her brother was playing by the roadway (which by the way was out of bounds to both of them). As my friend and I get close to the roadway we saw the boy run across the road and then sat down on it. Well !my friend yelled at him and started running towards him. Just as we got to him. The boy stood up and walked towards his dad. My friend was fuming at his sons actions and all of a sudden a car came around the corner and carried on. (Well we all know what would of happened if we had not found him

Before his dad could tell him off, the boy just looked at us and said Johnny said it is OK to play on the road because he knows when a car is coming. Who's Johnny said his dad. He's my new friend who came a few weeks ago

I then explained to my friend what was going on, and he then called out to the universe to take little Johnny away. That the universe did, Johnny was gone in one big flash of light and never seen at their house ever again.

So please to those who are reading this book and know of a similar situation please contact or inform a light worker. As some of those in spirit who have not been home to the light can be mischievous

Spiritual Guidance

To those who can speak to or listen and can hear your spirit guides please trust and have faith in what you receive. To those people who are just starting in this process please remember to check and double check that the messages are from those in the light and to check is to ask. If you receive no answer then tell them to move on. Also ask your guides' from the light to remove them from your space. I Thank my guides many times when I either go to the markets or shopping. I receive guidance where to park. An example, I was going shopping at the Robina Town Centre on the Gold Coast. One day I was in a line of cars going up the undercover parking ramp when all the parking space lights ahead turned red and a flashing light saying full. all the cars in front of me followed the arrow pointing to the left,as they all turned off and went to a different parking area. I received please listen. Just as I was about to turn left I received please go straight ahead. So I did all the car spaces were full so I thought okay I trust,then I received please slow down then slower and slower then I received please stop. Just as I stopped a car pulled out in front of me and drove off. In I went one very hand car park. Thank you

I replied I am very grateful. Not only did I get the car park. It was not far from the shops that I intended to go to please trust.

Guidance when sailing is also much appreciated not too long ago three of us were sailing a yacht down the east coast of Queensland Australia. We were sailing by day and then anchored at night in a nice quite bay at some island. After sailing for two days I received a message from my Spirit Guide, please do not stop at an island tonight please keep going through the night and you will see why tomorrow morning. So we kept sailing and (motoring when the wind stopped) through the night. I did wonder why as the weather forecast was for Light winds and sunny and fine for the next four days. Well the next morning came, a beautiful sunrise and hardly any wind with only a few clouds, also by where we were heading too. the other two people on the yacht were still asking why we didn't stop as planned at a very popular Island anchorage I just explained to them you will see in a few hours why (even I didn't know why except what I had heard from my Spirit Guides) They just looked at me and shook their heads. We sailed into a Marina at 8-30 in the morning and believe it or not at 9-30 am the wind changed direction. Blew 25-30 knots and by midday it was blowing continuous 30 knots and pouring with rain. Thank you I replied to my guides. The three of us on the yacht said 'Wow how lucky were we, just as well we sailed all night. As a gust of wind and heavy rain so heavy you could hardly see the other boats in the Marina

A few years ago I flew from Brisbane Airport to Auckland, New Zealand, on arriving in Auckland I decided to catch a bus from the airport into the city. Thought I might look around the city for a while, after a couple of hours I decided that I'd had enough of walking it was cold and overcast. I thought oh well Ill catch a train from Auckland to a town called Palmerston Nth so I went to the train station brought a ticket as it was leaving in three hours

About fifteen minutes later I was standing outside a travel shop, there was a billboard saying. Bus leaving to Wellington in twenty minutes. As this bus went via Palmerston North. I instantly felt take this bus and cancel the train. With this feeling I went back to the train station and asked for my money back. No worries was the reply it just cost me ten dollars to cancel. I walked back to the bus and off we went. about seven to eight hours later I arrived in Palmerston North. I got a bed for the night and when I awoke in the morning the main news on the radio and TV was that the train from Auckland to Wellington was derailed and the people were being taken by ambulance to the hospital. Guess what? that was the train trip I had just cancelled.

Lucky or what. Please trust in your inner guidance. Messages can come in many different ways

Spiritual Connections
& Intuition

All people have psychic capabilities and it can come to them in many different ways. How many times have you been working or driving, sitting at the table, or even engrossed in watching a program on TV when all of a sudden you get the urge to ring a certain person. You get up and go to the phone and just before you get there the phone rings. When you pick up the phone the voice at the other end is the person that you were just thinking of. Usually you just say to them, I was just thinking of you only a moment ago, they normally say that's funny I just felt like giving you a call all of a sudden. Well believe me it is not a coincidence as it happens a lot. It is a spiritual connection between us that we all have. Sometimes we act on it and other times we just dismiss it for whatever reason. The more you act and accept these connection moments. The more that they come to you. After a while you begin to pick up on a lot more than just a phone call. The reason I say connection moments is that many times they seem to come as quick as a flash and then gone. Quite often after one of these moments I sit and tune in on the message, but seems to be of no avail. Its like here's your message sorry you missed it but tough luck you're too slow better next time, be awake, or be aware more,so as a Word of Wisdom if you get any of these quick message moments, please act on them straight away and after a while you will notice that you receive a lot more, it is an exciting time.

Sensing and Seeing

Sometimes I get people ringing me up about certain scenes that they have just seen. It could be in their head, in a dream or that they just have sensed something so vivid it is like a picture. They usually explain about the good or not so good scenes that they have just encountered and would like to know what they can do about them. I usually explain to them, just be aware as some of these could take place at anytime. Watch TV or listen to the radio and take note if any of the scenes that you have seen or sensed comes to fruition (or happens) many times people have rung me up to let me know that they have just seen on TV what they had just seen a few days before it actually happened. One lady rang me one day and said that she was laying in bed awake when all of a sudden she saw in her head an aeroplane crash. She said the pilot was a blonde haired male who was in a panic because his aeroplanes motor had just stopped. Suddenly she said that she heard some of the words as he tried to start the motor, but to no avail. Also she said that the last words she heard from the male pilot was oh bugger this is it and then she saw it crash and nothing after that. I explained to her that I did not know the situation but please watch the news on TV.

About five days later I was watching the news on TV and there was the scenario that the lady had seen. It was a six seater plane with only the pilot on board. About two minutes later the lady rang in a panic. Did you see the news. Yes I did, was that the plane I replied. Exactly she said, I feel really bad I might have been able to help.

Well, I just said please relax there are hundreds planes like that in the air at all times and as you did not know where or when, who could you tell I am a firm believer if you were to help you would see the time and place. A few days later during a healing session the blonde pilot of that particular incident, came into my room in Spirit. He explained to me that the aeroplane had a fuel blockage and that he was now in the realm of Love - Light.

He said to me that where he was is more beautiful than you could ever imagine. But as with all others that I have spoken too. He said please do not try to get here just yet as it is not your time Love - Light Love - Light Love - Light and then he just disappeared. So my advice on this subject is also please be aware

Dreams

There are many books of Dreams/
Dreaming. I have been a dreamer
most of my life. Meaning I have
many dreams nearly every time I go to
sleep, day or night a very good idea is to
have yourself a dream book, or pen and
paper beside your bed, so that if you wake
up after or during a dream you can write
it down. Nearly every time that I wake up
and say to myself, Ill write it down in the
morning I forget what the dream was all

about. Many of the dreams are a part of us just sorting out everyday life

Also many of the dreams are a message from Spirit an example, if you are looking to buy a certain colour or type of car quite often you wake up in the morning with the urge to go out and buy a certain newspaper or to buy a certain car magazine. Most of the time if you act on this information, there is the car that you are trying to find, address, price, and all. Many people have explained this amazing gift to me over the years, and it has also happened to me on several occasions 'So my advice again is to please be aware'

Children Born With Psychic Abilities

Many children are born with psychic abilities, which confuses their parents. I have had many experiences where parents have said to me that their sons or daughters talk to themselves a lot (so they think) when I talk to the children myself they always deny that they are talking to themselves Actually in most cases they put their heads down and go quiet

When I explain to them that I also can see who they are talking to, they eventually lift up their head look straight at me and say, what's their name. Once I have said to them their friends name, they just open up and tell me what they talk about, how long they have been seeing them and where they came from. A person I know quite well. Who by the way is around sixty years old explained to me he had also seen and talked to spirit as long as he can remember. When he was a little boy he was always getting told off and punished for talking to himself. So off to his bedroom he was sent and told not to come out until he could be sensible well guess what, into the bedroom he would go and talk to his friend until they had talked enough. Then out of the bedroom he would come and then talk to his parents. This is an amazing story as his spirit friend was actually his twin brother who passed over at birth when he used to tell his parents the name of his spiritual friend, they just told him to stop being stupid, because your twin brother is not here anymore. So in the end he didn't tell anybody anything until he was a lot older and left home.

Now to the opposite approach I have had other parents who sit and talk to their children about the so called invisible children (remember, they are only invisible to some people) one lady explained to me how she used to tell her little girl off. But the little daughter used to insist about who she was talking to

So the mother one day sat with her daughter and asked all about the invisible friend and what the two of them used to talk about, after that the lady was so amazed at the different conversations she never told her daughter off again for talking to spirit. The daughter whom I have met is about 15-16 years of age now and very knowledgeable in Spiritual Awareness. The first time I met the daughter I was doing a bit of carpentry at their house. The girl came up to me and said. "You are a good Carpenter John and you know what to do properly, I looked at her and said thank you. I was a little amazed at how she spoke for a three year old and I just thought cheeky little thing. An hour later the grandmother called me for a cup of coffee. While sitting at the coffee table I explained what the little girl said. Oh that's because she was probably talking to her grandfather he was a carpenter when he was alive on the earth plane and the little one talks to him all the time, plus a few other relatives whom have passed on. With this I just smiled. About two years later I was talking to the little girls grandmother in her car. The little girl who happened to be sitting on the back seat lifted her head up and said you're a good healer John did you know there are angels everywhere.

So to the parents who tell your children off if they are talking to so called invisible friends, please remember these stories also please try to be a little more understanding and also it could be off benefit to all concerned if you could read some books or get on the computer to gather more knowledge on this subject and also of great advantage if you could contact someone in the spiritual field that can see and talk to those in Spirit. These stories are only a few of the many that I have come across

Animals

Many animals are aware of the other realms of existence. Have you ever been to your dog or to your cat just to have them looking right past you, or just above you totally oblivious to what you are saying. Most times they are looking at other beings in Spirit. Many people have explained to me, how they think that there favourite pet has come and visited them, even though their pet passed away many years ago. In some of their stories, people explain how they feel like their pet is walking on the bed and lays down in exactly the same place as when they were alive on the earth plane, by the persons feet or by their head, I see their pets in Spirit quite often and explain to them what I am seeing. Usually when I am explaining what and who I am seeing the people reply. That's my last pet or my pet I had when I was little, sometimes they say oh that's my parents pet which past away years ago. Sometimes I see pets all lined up in a row just waiting to be recognised. Often they turn up in Spirit with Uncles and Aunties pets as well. Sometimes plus the relative in Spirit as well. I have been lucky enough to talk to horses as well in their stables. On one occasion a particular racehorse kept trying to throw off its jockey by heading for the rail everytime it raced. The horses owner had been told by racing officials if the horse goes to the fence or to the rail one more time it will be banned from racing. The owner asked me if I could do anything about it. Well the horse explained to me that it loved the owner and also loved racing but did not like the jockey. When I asked the horse what was wrong with the jockey the horse replied, the jockey was a woman and it didn't want anything to do with a woman. The previous owner was a woman and she wanted to send it to the cannery for pet food, because it never won a race or even a place for that matter. The new owner was a male and when I told him this he burst all laughing. Guess what? he replied you are 100% correct. But we will see in a fortnight because the female jockey is going away for two weeks and a male jockey has been organised to ride it. I was talking to the owner of the horse about a month later and he explained that the horse got a second and a third in two weeks and that he had made some money for the first time with that horse. I don't know what happened after that as I never heard from him again.

Another time I was asked to go to a different stable and see if I could find out why a particular horse kept sprinting flat out at the start of each race, and about half way through the race couldn't be bothered running and always ended up last, when I went to go into the stable the trainer said please be careful as sometimes the horse doesn't like anyone that close. So I talked to the horse for a ten minutes and then I received a message come into the stable, which I just opened up the gate and to the trainers surprise the horse came up to me put its head on my shoulder like a long lost friend I put my arm around its neck and then asked it what it thought about racing. The horse replied. I like sprinting but not long races its boring. I would like to be a polo horse, and by the way please ask the trainer to change the food I only like Barley Oats and Hay. And also one more extra bucket of water every day. It then put its head under my shoulder cuddled into me and said thank you. I opened the gate and walked out. The trainer was Gobsmacked, it was like you were its best friend was the reply

I then explained to the trainer what I had been told she smiled at me and explained that's exactly how it races it goes to the front each time and races away then its like it gets tired and can't be bothered. Also about the food we feed it a very expensive mixed food and it blows half of it over the floor, so Ill try what you have just said. Two weeks later I went to the stables. The trainer said amazing it eats all of its food everyday, plus the extra bucket of water it drinks easily. Also the food now costs about a quarter of what it used to cost. about two months later I was talking to the trainer, she said that the horse got a third place and then the owner sold it to a farm in New South Wales where they play polo. And not only that the new owner thought it was the fastest Polo horse that he had. "Surprise surprise." Since then I have been to the stables just to say Hello.

Many times nearly every day in fact I talk or receive messages from animals, birds, fish, trees, (please remember everything that is alive can talk)

One day I was looking at some fairly big fish at a Marina. I crouched down on the jetty about a foot off the water, when I received you can stroke me if you like, I thought not with those big teeth I value my fingers too much. Wont bite was the reply so I leant over and put my hand beside this fairly big fish and stroked it from one end to the other. I did this a few times told it that I thought it was beautiful and then it just slowly swam away. Wow I said to myself, just love it, what a gift. Then I said to life itself Thank you.

Spiritual Experiences
and Critics

Many people have spiritual experiences and keep them to themselves for fear of being labelled as (fruit loops, nutcases, lost the plot, off this planet, what have you been taking, did you fall over and bang your head, what a load of rubbish, and many other sayings which rubbish someone else's experiences in life. To those people who ridicule other people like that (and by the way I get a fair few of those remarks also)

I normally say to them, do you know everything there is to know about everything in the Universe. The answer from them is always no I don't but that's ridiculous. So my next words are usually 'well don't rubbish what you don't know anything about,just because it has not happened to you as yet and may never will. Do not knock or rubbish anyone else's experience. There is a big difference in being a little critical than being a cynical know all. Most of the cynical people you cannot explain anything to them. So its best just to walk away. Those whom are a little critical usually listen to you while you are explaining and then remark. (Maybe, could be, seems a little way out, Actually I don't believe it). Quite a few people that I have met who have been critical about what I do have rung me over the years and asked what I thought about something that has just happened to them. By the time I've explained to them they quite often say well that's different I wont be so shut off next time.

Please remember all things are possible

Starting of Your Spiritual Experiences

Starting your spiritual experiences or being aware of this side of life. For a start everyone is spiritual because that is who we are. We are a Spiritual being having a physical experience on planet earth. Not the other way round. For many people this is very hard to comprehend but as one goes through the Spiritual Awareness and learning, we do seem to understand a lot more of who we really are. There are many ways of awakening ourselves. Some people through meditation some through Yoga, Development classes, Healing classes. Some with like minded small groups of others,some people through large established groups. Please remember what is great for some people, may not be very good for others. One thing that I have experienced first hand is that if someone running a certain group says to you that this is the only way, please give them a miss as they are not coming from the right space (mostly ego in fact) I feel that the best advice I can say is. If you feel comfortable with a particular way or group Go with it. Many people say to me that they have been to certain Spiritual learning groups and they feel very uncomfortable with the methods that they have been shown if it does not feel right please find another group. Your heart and stomach normally let's you know I personally myself have achieved a lot from meditation by myself and also a lot from many different classes. I went to many different meditation evenings, also many different spiritual healing classes plus Different Spiritual Development classes. Once I was asked to join a certain meditation and healing group. So I went along one evening and the first words that were said was Hello everyone this is a very special group, and this tonight you will be shown the latest and the only way to move to the highest spiritual achievement that you can. Well to me alarm bells went off straight away. Some of the other people went into wow mode, this will be amazing they said.

Well as I said earlier that type of talk comes from the human ego. So I did not say anything and went along with the night. What actually happened was a meditation first and then invoking a certain Coloured Light into the room. Then we all started sending healing to each other. Then with one person laying on a table the rest of stood around the healing table giving healing to that one person on the table. We all had a turn on the table and each one of us felt great at the end of the night. In actual fact it was just like many other healing nights that I have been to before. three of the ladies who where there had a beautiful energy coming from them and funny enough the least effective was the person organising the night (the one who said this was the latest way) the three ladies I mentioned could explain what they saw in a persons body and where the healing energy went and why. But the person who thought that he new everything never said a word, but was amazed at what was said by the three ladies. When I asked him what he saw and felt, he replied, nothing. I just do what I do, the more I discussed the night with him the more I realised that he was bluffing and was making out that he knew everything. He then went on to tell everyone that only a few people go to heaven, about a dozen.

Well that did it for me (my Spirit Guide was saying to me please don't say a word as the man who said that is slightly misinformed) I couldn't help myself and I then replied and I suppose you think that you are one of them. I hope so was the reply and then everyone said that they hoped so too. I stood up and said what about all of the other people in the world aren't they allowed. No, was his answer and with this I just replied you are full of it and then said Goodbye. Why I put in this story there are plenty of self confessed Guru's/Masters everywhere you go all over the world. So again I would just like to say. Please be wary and also go with your feelings of what feels right for you. Also their are many ways of learning about who we really are.

We are Love and Light beings and a part of us knows that we just need to be awakened on that subject. The right group or groups of people will be able to do that for you I myself learned much from many people and groups. Actually a certain amount of knowledge from each one I just sorted out what felt right to me and went along with that.

Tapping Into the
Universal Energies

Many people say to me after a session whether it be a healing session or a message from spirit session you must get really tired. No I do not is always my answer. I tune into the respective Universal energies and I work with the Love-Light in fact it enables me to do this type of work for many hours without getting tired. Before I start a healing session I always ask to be a pure channel for the Universal healing energy from the highest essence. Also when running a Spiritual class or an evening of Mediumship. I always ask for the messages that I receive to come from the highest realms of Love and Light. When doing this type of work I may be going for up to seven hours during the day and sometimes a few hours at night. By the end of the night I am wide awake and full of energy (to me it is a great space to be in) once I get home, still buzzing by the way, I can sit in the lounge talk-laugh and usually about an hour later that's it, ready for a good sleep. Tuning into the different energies is like tuning into a certain radio station. All things have a different vibration rate. You wouldn't tune into a talk back radio station if you would like to listen to music. And that is how the different universal energies are. To some of you reading this, you will understand as many of you probably have had already the experience that I have just mentioned, to others who try this, all it will take is to ask for the respective energies that you would like to be part of. One day something will happen to make you go Wow and from then on just go with your experiences. By the way we already are a part of all of these different energies, we just require to be woken up to that fact. And as I already have said once something amazing happens in your life while doing or asking for these energies. It can change your life, or the way you look at life forever. Please remember when asking for the Love and Light of all things.' That is what you get. (Please Trust.)

Many people that have come to me for a certain type of session comment on how many different colours that they see and how bright they appear to be. When having a session of mediumship often it can come as a flood of messages from friends or loved ones. So if you get yourself into this particular space it is of great value to ask the universe for order as it is not to easy to understand what is being said and by whom,you could end up with ten or more people in Spirit. Trying to talk to you all at once. There is nothing to be afraid of and they will not be offended. Once spirit has been home to the Light there is no judgement and they come to you with Love and Light they just would like to talk to you if possible. Myself I have three specific

Spirit Guides who organise the messages for me. To me they are the mediators between myself and to those who would like to relay a message. There is never anymore than One Spirit Talking to me at any one time. And I do thank them and Love them very much. They are pure love and Light also I have many other Guides and Helpers around me who are also pure Love and Light and I consider myself a very Lucky Man to have such light beings with me. Many people who come to see me that can also see spirit say Wow you do have many helpers with you. There are Light beings everywhere. Now and again I have had people say to me that my room and even the space around me inside or outside is lit up like a Christmas Tree. So to finish off this paragraph please ask the Universe for what it is that you are after simply because we are allowed to.

We are allowed to Laugh Sometimes

Many of the critics are quite amazing here is a few actual events

O   What do you do John for work

JN   I am a kinieseologist and also a Spirit Medium

What are they and what does that mean

JN Mediumship means that I talk to the spirit of those whom have past over, or past away, or died, which ever way you look at it

O I don't believe in that stuff its rubbish when we die we are just that DEAD in the ground we go goodbye

JN Well your father just said that you always were a doubting Thomas and just because it hasn't happened to you it doesn't exist

O Where did that come from

JN Your father he is standing beside you, he said he was a wood Turner, loved fishing and always had to have a good car. Also he said he is with you favourite uncle who used to take you fishing

O   Sounds like him because that's what he did when he was alive, you're kidding me you're having me on

JN   What about the Uncle

O   Yep that was dads brother he used to take me fishing Great Guy

JN   They both said that they love you very much. Keep up the project you're doing and don't worry about them as its more beautiful here than you could ever imagine but also don't try to get here just yet as it is not your time, also please ride carefully on the road

O   Well now you've got me thinking. How about I come and see you for a full session, see what else comes up

JN What's the story about riding carefully

O   I ride a motorbike and love going fast

,

O   And John what sort of work do you do

JN A Spirit Medium

O   What's that

JN I talk to Spirit of those who have passed away or passed over how ever you look at it

O   You mean died. You're another weirdo
they are everywhere I don't believe in
all of that rubbish don't even want to
know. Anyway if there was somebody
around me I would know wouldn't I

JN Well your best friend is beside you and
he just told me he got killed in a car
crash seven years ago and was sorry
about the tears he caused you, and also
he just said don't be so closed off to
things that you don't know

O   Go on

JN He said he was also your brother

O   Hey now you're scaring me

JN Why

O Because that's what happened to my best friend and I never had a brother. But everyone and also myself called him my brother

JN He said he is with you a lot and loves your boat also

O Now you're really scaring me I'm going weirdo.

JN You asked

O Yea I did now I suppose I have to believe because everything you said that is exactly how it was Goodbye

f

O What do you do John

JN A spirit medium

O   I've heard of them don't believe in it
    at all

JN I talk with spirit just like talking to you

O   Are you shore you're not a schizophrenic

JN Not that I know of why

O   Its all rubbish

JN No its definitely not rubbish

O   Prove it

JN Well you asked, your mother is beside
    you wearing what she is saying was and
    still is her favourite pink hat, its got a
    little pink bow on one side and also she
    is wearing a jacket of the same colour
    with short fluffy hair

O That sounds like her, how did you know, that's what mum always wore

JN I can see her and she just told me so

O Well what about my best friend that died several years ago fell of a staircase and died. Try that one.

JN You're friend just said in those days she was very stiffnecked type of person and now she is not. Also she is laughing about the stiffnecked story why would that be

O She landed on her head and broke her neck. Now you're making me cry

JN Well you did ask

O   I think Ill have to come and see you about a couple of others

JN   They just said they're ready and waiting and also looking forward to it. Also they said thank you for allowing yourself to change and believe, they are very humorous and are now making jokes

O   That's them you're making me cry

JN   Happy tears I hope

O   Yes they are thank you

"

O   Hello John pleased to meet you. My friend said that you talk to spirits.

That's pretty weird to me, but I suppose you can think whatever you like. Whether its true or not is a different story. I don't believe in it anyway. Just thought I would let you know.

JN You must love cats

O I do so what

JN There is a black and white cat in Spirit sitting in front of you

O So

JN Also there is a ginger striped cat beside you, and also a white cat with a black patch on one ear they are sitting there in Spirit

O   Well I've had cats fitting all those descriptions. So what

JN   Just letting you know that the spirit of those cats are with you

O   I used to talk to my cats you know and I know that they used to talk to me also

JN   They just that is correct but you never listened to what they said

O   What do you mean by that

JN   They used to say to you (and by the way there's a black cat with a big white patch on its forehead which said it is still alive in the physical its with you everyday and you don't listen to it either) what they are saying and are

trying to tell you is they like the food
Kitty Kat that you give them but they
do not like the other tin food at all but
you do not listen to them

O   Wow that is interesting because I feed
them Kitty Kat food in a tin and have
been doing so for years the Kitty Kat is
more expensive than the other tin food
and I have only ever bought the two
types. I usually buy the cheap brand
by the carton but only when it comes
on Special

JN They all said thank you for loving and
looking after them and they love you
very much

O   Well fancy that maybe I have learned
something today you are 100% correct

thank you. But I still think its still weird.

° ••• °

O   Hi John how are you going these days

JN   Good thanks and yourself

O   Fine I heard that you're into spiritual work, talking to spirit and also past life stuff

JN   Yes that's correct I find it absolutely amazing, what do you think about the subject

O   Well I reckon we are all spirits and I believe in past lives, does that surprise you

JN No not at all. Actually I just saw who you were in a past life, are you interested in knowing

O Okay go ahead

JN Well you were in the bottom half of Africa and a well known male by the name of ----- A total rebel raiding other villages and taking some of the woman with you. Sometimes you went up North and burnt villages and took some of their woman as well

I can see you plain as day, tall & fit, annoyed about something and also see you fighting the white man soldiers

O That's amazing I've read a book about him but I think that you are totally wrong because he didn't go up north at all So Wrong Guy.

JN How do you know about that

O Funny enough I've just come back from Africa and went to a lot of places and to certain villages where I have always wanted to visit. I actually felt like I had been there before but I wasn't him

JN Just letting you know what I heard and saw that's all (3 months later) a phone call

O Hey you might have been right I've just been reading about ----- on the computer, He did go up North with his people and raided villages, and set fire to them. Wow Amazing. Well I'm glad I am not like that in this life for to ruthless for me. But I know now why I always had an interest in that part of Africa and that particular person thanks.

✝

O   Hi Nanty (my nickname) haven't seen you around for a long time, what's up

JN I've been studying Kinieseology and spiritual healing so I haven't been out and about much for the last few years, what about you

O   Same as always but I have got this pain in my arm and I can't lift it above my shoulder height its been like it for about fifteen years

JN Maybe I can help in some way

O You're kidding me its a load of rubbish I've never been into that Mumbo Jumbo stuff, what made you start it all anyway

JN Its a long story but I do find it very interesting though

O Oh well each to their own I suppose so you think you can heal people do you

JN Well I can sometimes help them but I never guarantee anything in the way of results.

O Maybe your Mumbo Jumbo thing can help, Ha, Ha.

JN Well it started when you were in a certain high profile job and its got a lot to do with you playing around with the secretary at work. You got caught and got yourself into big trouble

O Go on

JN There is a lot of emotional energy that you are carrying with you regarding that particular incident

O Mmm smarty pants Ill tell you what happened. About fifteen years ago I was married and got caught playing around with the secretary from work. I'd had an affair with her for about eighteen months. When I got caught my whole life changed. My wife left me, so did the secretary, and also I left my job. It was a pretting emotional and hard time (all my fault of course) but what's all that got to do with my arm

JN All that emotional energy with that story is bottled up and stored in your left arm. Believe it or not give me your left arm to hold for a moment if you like and well see what happens

O   Okay its weird actually but funny enough its feeling better already

JN Well that's all for now how about coming around home in a weeks time for half an hour or so 3 months later

I met him in a shopping centre. Hey how are you going

O   Good thanks Nanty what about you

JN Good thank you how come you didn't come around home the week after I saw you last

O   I told you I wasn't into that Mumbo Jumbo stuff. Anyway I didn't need to come and see you because my arm came right by itself about a week after I saw you

JN That not bad is it, you had it for fifteen years and then it went by itself a week after you saw me

O   Yep so I didn't bother to come around, look I can even lift my arm straight up in the air. No pain its great. What else have you been doing lately Nanty

JN Sailing.

✣

O   Hello John a friend of mine came to see you and was totally amazed at the messages that she had received, so she recommended that I come to see you. So here I am

JN How might I be able to help

O   I feel that I have a Spiritual blockage and hopefully you can clear it

JN Well do you believe in Past Lives

O   Certainly I have seen myself in many lifetimes

JN I am getting that you were an excellent healer and a very good psychic many lifetimes ago

O   I know

JN Well what happened you made up a lot of stories which were untrue but at the time made you quite famous

O   I know who I was

JN So in this lifetime you are to tell only the truth its a karmic reaction.

O   Well that's funny because I am a psychic now and I do readings everyday and

also I keep getting the message myself
(Truth Truth Truth)

Also I just got told to be quite and to
listen to what is being said by you and
my blockage will be cleared

JN I just received that you do tell the truth
and do not make up stories to fill in
the time. This is why you receive more
information than many others in your
field.

O I just received for you to put one hand
on my forehead and one hand over my
stomach

JN I thought you just got asked to listen

O Sorry

JN Well I also received a message one hand on the top of the head and one hand over the heart are you OK with that

O Whatever – Wow a brilliant light of many different colours just went through me. Brighter than anything I have ever seen before

JN That's it you're finished blockage cleared

O You've got to be kidding – just like that

JN Yes that's all

O Well I tell you I am getting messages given to me by my guides clearer and quicker than ever before. I went to ask a question and received the answer before I even asked. Also the pictures I am seeing are brighter and clearer than ever before the colours are amazing

JN That's good then I hope it makes you happy

O By the way you are going to teach also be on stage talking. And doing lots of other things that you never thought that you would be doing. Thank you for that

Goodbye got to go.

IZ

I can relate to all of these stories as I am Johns guide. So please trust and one will see what lies ahead right throughout the universe. Also the Universe is changing always like what you have never seen before and also I can verify that the God of Love and Light will shine brighter than ever before Love and Light to you all, and that is all.

John W. Nant

John can be contacted on

61412926916

Queensland Australia

EMAIL johnwnant@optusnet.com.au

Printed in the United States
By Bookmasters